EXCEPT WE TEACH

Alan Gillott

EXCEPT WE
TEACH

Alan Gillott

Fighting Cock Press

Published by
Fighting Cock Press
45 Middlethorpe Drive
York, YO24 1NA

ISBN: 978-0-906744-44-4

Printed and bound in the UK by ImprintDigital
Original Fighting Cock Logo by Stanley Chapman
Cover design by Alan Gillott
Images courtesy of NASA and Roberto Sorin

Edited by Pauline Kirk

Author's Note

Finding a title for a book, or collection is not easy. It has to suggest something of what the book is about, entice the reader, and not be a hostage to fortune. Picking one of the poems is one method; this led to the selection of *Beyond the Window* for my first collection. The working title for this collection (which I will not repeat here) was appropriate for the original draft before my Editor, Pauline Kirk, got hold of my poetry database and turned everything on its head. She also thought that the putative title was indeed a hostage to fortune, or more to the point, only too exploitable by a witty reviewer's pen. My next inspiration was to pick yet another poem from the collection, *Between the Lines*. Looking beyond and between is a theme for my poetry and writing: what is it about life that is risky, or dangerous, or even wonderful or joyful. I flirted with *Under the Carpet* or *Behind the Wardrobe* or even *Under the Egg* keying on the first in the sequence of Keats' poems. In the end, in these troubling times I selected a line from 'The Egg': *Except we Teach*.

Once again I must thank Pauline Kirk, my editor, for lifting the book from the banal to the singular. An editor looks at poems dispassionately, ignoring the personal baggage that might be inhibiting. A poem is a very different form of writing to short stories or novels, having a much greater emotional component. An editor has no investment in any of my poems so is able to make a more reasoned selection than I. Philosophers will argue the emotional basis behind reason but at the very least they are not my emotions or prejudices. The editor therefore is in a much better position to expose my predilections untrammelled by censorship. Thank you once again, Pauline.

Also by Alan Gillott and published by Fighting Cock
Press

Beyond the Window

Acknowledgements

Some of the poems printed here have previously been
broadcast, or appeared in the following journals and
anthologies:

*Iraq 1: Tosca; Iraq 4: Cocky; Bleak Blake; A Little Prose
Poem*; *Real; Luxury; Land With Opportunity; What Will I
Remember*   Broadcast by Eden Agency programme: The
Poetry Show
Five Days After   Poems for Peace online Project, Ohio
University
Liminal   Dream Catcher 30, Stairwell Books
Keats' House, Rome   Broadcast by York University Radio
Land With Opportunity   Featured in print *Intersecting
agriculture* by Catherine Sutcliffe-Fuller and a glass
etching by Steve Bowen in an Exhibition entitled *Land
With Opportunity,* the etching now in the possession of
Dean Clough, Halifax.

Contents

Scarborough

Scarborough
In the twenty-first century
Is coloured by sepia memories
And silver nitrate browns
Whose edges curl
With faded sharp
Images
Captured by a Box Brownie brain
Untrammeled by politics
Of family
Or filtered by experience
By love
By loss
Distorted by events
Corrected by necessity
Or edited for effect
Snapshots needing no caption

The car, black cracked leather and melamine
Filled with aunts and cousins,
Driven by Uncle Frank
Who drove his empty coach to family events,
Or Uncle Billy, or Victor
One of the many Crookes
From Totley and Dore
Naked knees between Nannan Connie
And Auntie Hilda
Mind frozen with unanticipated expectation...

Then
Suitcases
The Landlady, we appear to know
From last year and the year before,
The sands
Donkeys
Or is that from Margate or Blackpool?

Jelly and Ice Cream
Paddle boats in a great park lake
Fifteen inch steam railway
The driver seated on the tender
Hunched over the controls
Denim flat cap with railway badge
And the persistent little boy
Who wants to ride again
Again!

That same little boy
Returning
Shooting in high density digital colour
Tries hard
So very hard
To turn the album back
To grow the pond into the remembered lake
To clamber again up upon that train
To cast his clout upon the sand
Run free and bare
Wishing the bright faced houses
Return to grey
With coal soot and smuts
Captured
In memorial sepia
Welcome to Scarborough ‹

Iraq 1
Tosca

His name was Tosca
This two tone brown
Ironic gelding proudly
Seating a six year old boy
Taught on the bare back
Of indolent obdurate donkeys
Picking a never repeated path
Amongst fat tailed sheep
And assertive ragged goats

Schooled to ringside rigour
This misplaced beast
Responsive to gentle touch
And delicate heel
Trotted and cantered
With unerring precision
And snorting pride
That the donkey boy now knew
What a real horse could do ‹

Iraq 2
Joseph

His name was Joseph
From the hills above Beirut
But he was here in the hills
Above the desert in the camp shop
Selling sauces and sugars
Soap, string, and shoelaces
To those everyday engineers' wives
Plucked from bucolically prim English lives
To live on the hill still above
Where the resident engineer drives
Chez toutes les jours tout le monde femmes
Avec les voitures de Peugot et aussi Citeöen
On a hill above the yet empty dam
Where the Lesser Zab flowed to the Greater Zab cold
Tumbling through coffers and piling
While Joseph
Crouched
By a spigot
Spiked through a dark shiny oil drum
Shows a seven year old boy
How to cut arak
Into used screw cap beer bottles
For sale to the Kurds
Who live in this place ‹

Iraq 3
August 23rd 1957

His name was Mamakaal
Sheik Mamakaal
It was his people
Losing limbs and lives
On the growing face of the great dam
And their hearing in the tunnels
To the turbines
And whose fields would be drowned
In the flooding lake
Now large enough to feature
On a school room world map

Wherever anybody went
So went Mamakaal
And to day was Margery May's
Birthday picnic on a pebbly reach
Upstream where the waters chilled
The beer and the children swam
To spite the heat
And the birthday cake
In pride of place on a trestle

Even the little boy, well supplied
With never-heard-of-before Coca-Cola
Was allowed to drink the lager
And by the time the sausages
And kebabs were ready
The evening chill brought out the brandy
And Mamakaal had sat on the cake

What no-one then knew
Was the cake baked on a primus
With paraffin
Fractioned from the oil of Kirkuk
An extra polluting ingredient

And Mamakaal the wanted unwanted
Was feted by Margery May
Because he, Mamakaal, saved the day ‹

Iraq 4
Cocky

His name was Cocky
Cocky was a partridge
The last of a line of pets
Which included a cat
And a mongoose

Cocky was free to roam
From room to room
A frequent visitor of arm
Of shoulder or knee
And on a lazy day
Would hitch a ride
On a convenient toe

Then came the day
When the job was done
And we would all go home
What to do with Cocky?

Cocky could stay with cook
Or up the hill with Joseph
'Till his feathers grew out

In the event, our last meal
In the mountains
Was partridge stew ‹

India
Chowringee Market

Dark chaos and clatter
Mark bright lit clutter
Trip feet and hands; chatter
Cuts vendor from buyer; utter
Tumult rends rainbow matter
Ripening in cascades to gutter
Flow of aromatic splatter
Ground flat feet aflutter
Flay the pavement: dogs no fatter
Than beggars pause paws out stutter
Need. Passers savour sample flatter
The senses of abundant butter
Ghee of rupees, pice and annas
Silver rub of peas and spiced bananas ‹

The Shoplifter Cycle i
The Shoplifter

Outside the air is clear and bright
While here within the sickly stench
Of cloying perfume dims the light
And makes the atmosphere of treacle quench
The heart of blood which having bled
Swells to fill the chest with lead.

Each turgid step upon the floor
Seems to be viewed by all who see
As like a beacon through the store
A universe that fear creates through me:
An aura lighting all the air around
While in my breast each breath is drowned.

The moment comes when garments, lockets,
books, a silken scarf and fine ceramic boat
Are deftly placed into the secret pockets
So newly sewn into a fashion coat
Designed to give a lie to this profession
Pushed by a need to have possession.

The time has come to leave this place
Yet undue haste to escape the racks
Of clothes, adrenaline upon the face,
Will let the watchers know, the packs
Whose job it is to watch the floor
For goods unpaid to never reach the door.

So then with overburdening relief
To leave the stink of perfumed sweat
And stand outside, the sated thief,
To walk with dignity from threat
Imposed by those from whom I flee;
"Excuse me, Madam, please come with me." ‹

The Shoplifter Cycle ii
The Store Detective

There is Monday and Tuesday and Wednesday too,
Long hot languid days; long tiring, yawning,
Waiting, watching days; long standing, walking,
Seeing, hearing, waiting, watching Thursday Friday days.

Saturday's a busy, bustling, rushing hither thither day,
Peeking, glimpsing, seeing, hearing, walking, watching,
Shopping, buying, eating, darting, sitting, staring
Getting slowly bored, waiting until Sunday day.

Waiting over, face and quarry flushed on tempting floor
Of bright and tinsel, shining trinkets, reds and greens
And golden hues, those clothes of russet, mauve and
sherwood
Skirts and blouses, stands the hands of a shopping thief.

Now the covert signal, a practiced flicker not to wreck
The chance of capture: casual slow traverse across the
floor,
The tensing tightening in the stomach, head and neck,
While with imperceptible nod a colleague blocks the door.

Turned, observing from the corner of a watchful eye,
A ring, a pair of gloves, some silken scarves
All vanish into black mawed swaggering bag
While up above the flirting eye with unsuspecting
salesman laughs.

Then the long slow unsuspecting walk around the store:
Averting suspicion; a distance from the crime
Of theft, so deftly done, so almost undetected.
A drift toward the exit, escape, but not this time.

The dreams I often have of frightened, pleading eyes;
Round pupils, begging, misty, tearful, crying, greeting orbs:

The stories true and false; the desperate haunting tales, excuses;
Pale, shaken, vacant people, abused, reviled, rejected folk.

Not professional, these we never catch, only deter,
Not even amateurs, not knowing why or what they do,
Taking, stealing, hoping to be caught, yet frightened by the stigma,
Shoplifter, thief, outcast, out thrown, rejected.

Delivered to the hands of omniprecient law, they leave,
The forms filled in, the bonus paid, the high now over,
We the store detectives settle to the rhythm of the observation cycle,
There is Monday and Tuesday and Wednesday too... ‹

Love Story

Bless me father for I have sinned:
I have told a lie and deceived my wife;
My love, which eats the curdling heart
Of trust and stills the life of love.

This deceit is not of indiscretion
Nor of unfaithful spouses:
These are truths cured by cathartic pain;
Absolved by time and faith and hope.

This little lie, unheeded lie
Growing unseen and hidden
With cancerous intent masesticising
Throughout the tissue of our lives.

This little lie founded with intent
To heal my love and save her life
To comfort love and cherish
'Till the hand of time takes us from this life.

This little carcinomic lie;
The hope that heals the head and heart
That sets the attitude that cures
The oncogenic cell.

That cruel cellular indiscretion,
That slight genomic error
Excised, irradiated and abused,
A chemotherapeutic hell.

And yet, I have to say, believe: "You're cured"
While in my lonely heart I fret and fray
And wonder what our boys will feel
If only just one cell escaped?

Each day, each hour, each minute,
That divisive gulf becomes more real to me
Than all the precious drops of Lazarus' cooling balm
And all because of me; my breach of trust.

"This little lie I cannot share with you
This little breach of trust to save your life
Is killing me – This sin of loyalty
To you, for life, for love."

Bless me Father: I have sinned. ‹

Insinuation

The lies that hurt are not the ones we tell:
They, with grace, can be forgiven,
However much we have to lie to sell
The lie we told: we are still shriven.

The lies that hurt are not the ones that hurt
The ones we love: from them contrition:
More the stratagems that flirt
With truth and so rely upon omission.

The lies that really hurt the soul
Insinuate themselves into our hearts
And gently, without herald, take their toll
Upon the fabric of our lives with hidden parts.

This is the lie you have to live from day to day
Because your love to live must live a life of optimism
While deep within your heart you cannot but play
The scene of life taken from the book of carcinogenic
schism.

This is the lie the celibate must face
From day to day in loving homage
To the lives they cure and propagate
The fecund love of wedded bondage.

This is the lie of duty's child,
That follows in the path of parent's part:
A play from which their act beguiled
Destroys their life, their love, their heart.

This is the lie that makes the bate
That finds its way into curmudgeon's heart,
That fatal foetal lie for which we cannot legislate
But which we must beware: It must not start ‹

The Lie -
That Lie!

My love is the heart
In which I start
To tear apart
A life: my art. ‹

Disappearing Magic

There is no magic anymore
The touch that once quivers
The tingling tips of tiniest hair
Now triggers repellent shivers
Of pain politely hidden, I dare
Not share anymore

There is no magic anymore
In talk, or in simple presence
Shared, the gift of trust
Absent in a tense pretence
Rigid knees and chest, I must
Not share anymore

There is no magic anymore
The harm so long received I fear
Inflicted now on you, days filled
Conscious of unconscious scald will sear
Another little bit of me be stilled
Not shared anymore

There is no magic anymore
No anticipation expectation
But unfulfilling desert plain
My eternal commination
That I can no longer feign
To share, anymore ‹

Bleak Blake

What if all this
This that we see
This that we touch
This that we are...

What if all this
Were but a figment
Of a man's
Eidetic imagery

What if all this
Gravity light energy
Sprang from nothing
In the blink of an eye

What if all this
Were to fade away
Like the memory
Of a vivid dream

What if all this... ‹

Evening Calm

I walked out late in the evening balm
Light flitting warm across the streets
Darkening avenues evening calm
While heart of babbling New York beats

Here and there a cavernous courtyard
A private space of shade
That never sees the light at noon
Where steamy nights the invisible moon
Looms over lovers tight brocäde
Entwined behind the iron facàde

The myriad islands rushing slowly by
Aware ignoring flowing slips
Slip past the yellow stream of cars
Stuttering standstill flickering bars
Prepare for lonely isolate hips
To hitch a ride with convenient guy

As darkening green heralds night
When mothers, children leave the street
To lovers and loners: the luminous darkness
Of city light lines the starkness
Of the lambs; cars that bleat
As they follow one another out of sight

The beating slows before the dawn,
That city stasis, that pre-storm calm
That moment when the sun just tips the morn
As I stroll home in the morning balm. ‹

Silence

There is silence and there is silence
Where piece by piece the waves of life
Flow and overflow in unsteady rhythm
Unlike the relentless assault of sense
While nonsense beats with reverberating strife

Suburban silence sounds deep presence
Where random voices rustle and clatter
Ebbing and flooding with unsteady beat
Of fluttering cabbage white wings whence
Sparrow and starling and cicadas chatter

Bucolic silence swirls with busy absence
Where the mind of man carved and chipped
Back and forth an unsteady strum
Harvesting unseen rich abundant provenance
Day by day the hay unheard is clipped

Dumb silence screams out loud of violence
Where every word not ever spoken
To and fro over unsteady throb
Of painful witness to this last offence
Motivated still by standing silence unbroken

Then that fixed everlasting silence
Where each eternal atom leaves no trace
Here and not here an unsteady wave
Observed by ever-changing latent conscience
For penance howls aloud and fails to face
The inner quiet that signifies real recompense ‹

Perhaps

Perhaps
All it would have taken
Would have been
To have come to see me
To have put back on the table
Your abuse by your father
And by inaction your mother
And I would have made an effort

Perhaps
This was why you went out of your way
To provoke me
To make me hit you
But I did not
So you never believed that I loved you
Nor learned of love without pain
Or of the need for affection
Or touch

Perhaps
If you had told me
It might have been different
Or even acknowledged the damage
This had done to our marriage
I would have made an effort

Perhaps
I was done reaching out
Rebuffed and belittled
Reduced and rejected

Perhaps
It might have been mended

Perhaps
It might not

It never will now ‹

While Harry Expounded on the Dynamics of Poetry

"Occupancy of more than 104 persons is dangerous and unlawful on premises" read the Devil as he descended on the crowded premises at the Peacock Café. In consequence, and in accordance with the laws of the City of New York, he turned around and tempted somewhere else. ‹

Manhattan Storm

Firecracker lightning flayed
Pinnacles of the drowning city
Frackeling fearsomely close
As citizens scurried or clustered
Into or out of the squalling rain
Each cursing the other as coursing
Rivers drench unwary feet
Pinballing between scything umbrellas
Street furniture and blind traffic
Oblivious to shops or shoppers
Sex, age, colour, class or shape
Intent only on wetness or dryness
Shivering in the unaccustomed cold
Of the once warm washed street
Or the over air-conditioned stores
Unused to crowds of guilty shoppers
Pretending to browse for goods unwanted
Buying serendipitous treasures
Stored in fragile paper sacks
To be safely toted home through
The driving rain, off duty taxis
And the still frackeling lightning ‹

One of Those Avenues

Like a canyon on a hazy day
Lights changing strict in lock step
Measure the headlong rush of cars
From pools to rapids in regimented flow

In between the ants of men delay
On stepping stones they find adept
To dart between the line that scars
The canyon floor and find the caves below

Concrete adobe homes give way
To brilliant light of great concept
Where theatres share the walls with bars
Interspersed with pornographic glow

Where after you have been to see the play
Then flowed toward the end where's kept
The places best to eat and view the stars
To meet the people you really want to know

Downtown the weight of island granite grey
Breaks up the streets where planners wept
To see such crazy zig zag mars
Where the men of money lay down low

For at the very bottom the proud display
Of green as if from nature crept
Into the concrete steel formed jars
To remind us all how verdure grows ‹

A Little Prose Poem

I have never quite been able to discover how it was that I became a member of the oldest profession. To the best of my recollection, it wasn't until the priest and astrologer got together that anyone knew that my body was sufficiently valuable to sell. Until then, all I was doing, was having bloody good sex ‹

Futility

Futility
Waiting to be called
Carrot cake in hand
In a new age coffee shop
For a simple large black coffee

Inanity
Waiting while knowing
That scorching air
And scalding water
Means Mocha Vente Latte ‹

Gallette De Bison

"Gallette de Bison"
Proclaimed the sign

"Saveur Choix Naturel"
Of grass clad plains
With humpbacked beasts
Against azure gels
Of halcyon summer

Enthralled, I traced these words
Enticing them close, anxious
To see beyond. Savoring their touch
I turned them right around to read
"Buffalo Burger – Natural Choice Flavor" ‹

Open Heart

You touched my heart
In many little ways
You tugged at every tendon
Twisting every chord in knots
Until each beat was lost
In passageways I'd never seen before.

This is not the touch of love or lust
Nor that of hair or skin or tongue
But raw, uncooked, ungarnished touch
Of heart, now cut and sliced and diced
And chopped and ground into a paste
So sweet: a sauce in which
Mine own pulsates, alone.

Unworthy heart that talks to you
Of life – a life it cannot touch
Unless by feeling you and your
Beating, growing, yearning, giving heart
Which shares your pain by touching
My unworthy inner self

I am enhanced
You touched my heart
In many little ways
And now I wish to gouge it out
And knead it into bread
To share again, again, again
With others who have not tasted yours.

In many little ways
You touched my heart
I am enhanced by you. ‹

Pittsburgh

A gentle place
The bumpy hills
Bespattered, frame house littered.
A Spanish port?

There is no sea,
Basalt columns built
Bound, histogrammatic, set
Between bejewelled rivers.

A city of steel,
Bridges, dark steps, cut
Aquatic staircase corridors,
Stretched arms so far.

This sleeping behemoth
On human scale
Dwarfed by cliff, balanced,
The point from which it grew.

A promontory,
Forest, farmed and fortified
Formed between river and hill;
A muddy flooded frontier town.

The craft of man
Fueled by coal and wood and iron,
The smelter's sacrifice
Founds the city's core.

Those men of steel
Who built in stone an empire,
Not of states and kings,
Whose soul is buried here.

We stand humble, beneficent,
Bereft of foundry, mill and grime,
In awe, amazed so much is left unspoiled:
This city, Pittsburgh, preserved for human kind. ‹

Five Days After

Smoke stained picture postcard blue
Sky yet tranquil over Manhattan
Island surrounded by white capped
Wavelets of Mediterranean water
Cut by speeding leisure boats lapped
Picturesque quays and scenic view

This calm is the calm from which grew
The still voice of God still small
Enough to envelop each stricken heart
And murmur to each suffering soul besieged
By beleaguered reason for grief to start
To wash corrupting hatred's gangrenous stew

Tear's rivulets reform in dusty flue
White smoke in purity translates each spirit
Wrapped with foreshortened brilliant dreams
The which we who mourn our duty now
Is sweet revenge to see these schemes
Fulfilled and every soul receive their due

The setting sun a bloody crimson hue
Reminds us every day to pray once more
And whisper to the wind each sacred name
Whose nature is to carry swirling sound
Rustling reeds and rushing mountain to where shame
Will ever bloom and also for petals in their path to strew ‹

Done

Done
In the twinkling of that eye
At a stroke
It is done
In that one moment a suspicious
Immigration officer damns the lives
Of three good people
One to gaol
One to pain and physical hurt
And the other, a child, to anguish
At the impending absence

Three full hearts emptied
Condemned to stare at the empty hearth
Wasting their sweet love on officials
And make work documentation
Just to bring that one heart
Home again to love day by day

It is done
At a stroke
In the twinkling of that eye
Done ‹

Bittersweet Goodbye

Light lingers on your sleeping form
As the morning sun sneaks through
The motel curtain illuminating
Each hill and dale of your resting face

Yet this long week's self inflicted storm
Our idyllic love with wreckage strew
And knowing time is short together
I map every memory of this face

In love and care and pain reform
And those lines in anger drew
So soon erased for me and Em
Yet at rest so sweet your glowing face

These memories will be the norm
For a little in which I get to rue
My self defeating shame
Remembering your ever changing face

But now the sun so nearly warm
Touches you for me again so new
My heart is caught again to catch my eye
Determined to return to touch your face ‹

Watch

I have my watch on your time
And from so far away can watch
My life pass as it should have been
Watching you with curb and care

I have my watch on your time
To within my mind's eye watch
Em watch her morning scene
And watch her to the bus with care

I have my watch on your time
To any instant know to watch
You rise with pain so keen
And watch you wash and brush your hair

I have my watch on your time
To know when for the bus to watch
And be aware of the returning teen
From school to watch for life unfair

I have my watch on your time
Sensing when you start to watch
The things we share upon the screen
And in my sleep I watch you in our lair

I have my watch on your time
Because in my dreams I watch
You sleep curled up to glean
My warmth as I watch you bare ‹

Touch

Of all the things I miss of you
Your strength and sense and smell
Your voice and nearness close
Is touch
I crave that fleeting touch of you
In passing by or being near
Or close together on the couch
We touch
So many times of every day do you
In some way touch my hide or heart
My arm, my back, my hip or face
You touch
The very essence that I am to you
That when apart my skin dims down
Because it fears to never feel again
Your touch
But when once more I'll be with you
We'll feel each other close as one
And reassure our craving skin
That we're together ever more
In touch ‹

31

Morning Walk

As summer slips away to fall
The autumn sun framed by still green trees
In the dew damp air, a big red ball,
As the fresh pink sky flees
Replaced by silver grey wisps of cloud
And skeins of white on blue

Fresh from touching you, so far
Away, in sweet caressing words
And drinking your oh so real attar
While this spasming heart girds
My essence close to expend in you
When we are to touch for real

I walk, spirit raised, in the fresh
Morning air still chilled by night
Paths and ponds steaming as our flesh
Will shimmer at our first sight
Of each other when we meet
After too many days and nights apart. ‹

Subway Stairs

It was dusk and raining
Which is not especially unusual
Except that this was the first rain in a long while

My Rose and I were walking home
Hand in hand happy in the rain
Speckled our spectacles scattering
Headlights and street lamps and occasional star

When without a care in the world
Came the fox or maybe vixen
To pause at the subway stairs
And for one long beautiful moment
We marvelled at this perfect sign
Our daughter's spirit guide
Stared back, pointed face, bushy tail,
Relaxed until the twenty first century
Took us over, we reached for the camera
And the fox continued her routine
Using the subway to cross the road
Just as its designers intended ‹

Moon Over Santa Domingo

I see you precious moon that smiles
On Croydon town so clear tonight
That silver glow that tames the sun
And bathes still water's silver sheen
Or glitters on the breeze's ripples
Making river's flowing eddies glister
Bringing dark to life and light to night

I see you smiling on the sea glowing
In the wakes of ships and whales grinning
From the caps of breaking waves to wrest
A grin from grim and grizzled faces
Melting hearts which on any other day
Would turn the Gorgon back to stone
And scare away the fiercest winter storms

But best of all I see your beaming smile
Upon the face of my delight alas alone
Asleep maybe or sleepless dream of me
Bathed together by that self same silvern light
Stirring the breeze through the palm fronds
And memories of mirrored lakes and glowing mists
As she lies alone in the moonlight in Santa Domingo ‹

Parisian Painting

It is a tiny unremarkable
portrait of a not so young woman
not quite smiling
as if I were naked

She pensively remarks
on all those cold marble statues
tastefully reduced
for maiden eyes ‹

Missed

It is early; and cold
Smoke from smokeless fuels
Drifts down into the clinging mist
Joining acrid early morning
"I'll leave my engine running
because I don't care about my neighbours"
Fumes spread like dry ice
Over the still damp pavement

The sun, a glowing daytime moon
Hovers, failing to warm
Enough air to make a breeze
Sufficient to scour away the mist
Or corrupting leaden taint
Compound by leafless trees
And bastion homes warding the roadside
Sentinels against some other harm ‹

A Little Bit of Me

A little bit of me died today
somewhere, somehow, something
did not happen that should have happened
and that package which is me
is not the same

To look at me you see the same
hair, mouth, eyes, frown;
the voice is just as you remember
that quiet reassuring calm
is just the same

But, just the same, there's something not quite right
There's a nagging in the corner of *your* mind,
a something you cannot quite, quite put your finger on
and cannot quite compose the words to ask
that question you know I cannot answer
I see it too, reflected back to me
because I know the truth.

A little bit of me died today
just like that bit from yesterday
and another bit tomorrow
I see the horror of this endless slaughter
I cannot stop, laid out
these body bags of me,
piled so carelessly together
because the bit that cared died too

A little bit of me died today
an accelerated apoptosis
of the essence that looked to you
sustaining life, the love now gone

I scramble through the bags
to try to see which bit I lost
but each resembles you:
your hair; mouth; eyes; frown;
no voice, there is no breath in death
because each little bit of me is really you
and as you slip away from me
I slip away from you
until we're neither there

No more

We cannot let this happen evermore?

A little bit of me died today. ‹

I Cannot Just Stop Loving You

I cannot just stop loving you;
that will never change;
you'll never just be just my friend;
or even just a close friend;
but my friend and lover,
because I know you are. ‹

Hubris

Hubris is a hanging offence
Or some other form of lingering fate
By fire or flaying or fearsome beast
In a public place to discourage us all
From straying away from common humility

But also is heresy!

To be a heretic requires that someone
Determines with absolute certainty
The inviolate Word of God
And that every word of scripture
Is the only truth and the hand of God
Never teaches through art or science
And the condom is the spawn of the devil
And thousands of women should be
Condemned to death – denied access
To reproductive health
That it is God's plan for humanity
To founder on overabundance

Is this not Hubris, a hanging offence? ‹

Shame

Each bomb may speak to you
Of triumph and one more tiny step
For freedom and the right to rape
And kill in the name of Allah

Whose tears wash clean the faces
Of those who died as He Himself
Takes their hand and leads them
To stand in honour on Her right

Yet each and every bomb and body
Advances by an hour, a day, a year
That moment when the voice of Arab woman
Will be heard aloud abroad

And the right of man to force
On pain of death a woman's pride
Will be no more a part of Arab lore
And a frail remembrance of human shame

Void

There is a void
into which I cannot fall
nor yet be pushed
beside which I stand
holding your hand by the fingertips
as you teeter at the edge of your chasm
unsure whether to take that step
or wait for the straw wind
of fate to tip your balance
into inevitable oblivion

My void will come to me unbidden
Filling the vacuum left by my side
With bitter sweet reminiscence
And my certain promise to you and your child
My longing for your company
Fulfilled by your lifetime of words
And the joy of my wardenship
But you will not be there to share
With us the days of sorrow

Be strong my love
hold tight that together we can resist
the wind with strength between
our fates ˄

Telecommunion

In the morning I awaken aware
Of you so close to me
That I turn to embrace the space
By my lonely side
My arm draws in the air
Fragrant with your sweet smell
That tastes so sweet
I settle comforted enclosing you
Cloaked in my dream of us
Together

When we next speak
I hear you tell me
How when you went to bed
My spirit self enfolded you
Held you so close to taste
And smell my clasping arm
While my nearby warmth
Took away the chill of night
Cloaking you with dreams of us
Together ‹

Real

Last night my hand explored
Your curves remembering
Every crevice of your golden skin
Each bone and tendon, knot and chord
My fingers teased and rolled
Each painful nub and followed
Every muscle to its source
Deep inside your pain wracked core.

How different from the touch
Of your eidetic self I know so well
Willed by you and I in bed together
So far apart, your night, my morning, dream
Of you or I combined conspire
Bizarre reality right next to me
Your smell, your touch, your breath, your warmth
Curved so close to relieve your pain
Enclosed within my arms and thighs
As you too enfold me close

Last night I really touched each nerve
Remembering every knot, each point of pain
And pleasure
While you untrammelled
By this tender exploration
Remained asleep assured of love;
I listened to your rhythmic breath
So soft and reassuring
Remembering every moment, every movement
Every sound and every smell
For tomorrow, to be together,
We must be our eidetic selves again ‹

I Have Been There

I have been there
Strolling arm in arm
With Destiny
Knowing nothing
Only everything
Seeing the white light of Chaos
And the black of absolute order
Where ethereal progressions
Introduce discordant absence

Yet throughout this display
of seductive irresponsibility
and thankful relief
glowed undiminished
my eternal image
of You
changing but constant
present and absent
cut through the crystal clouds
reached through sweet despair
took my hand and drew me home
to you

I came back ‹

Between the Lines i
Joseph

Were Joseph poor or humble
He would never have been in Bethlehem
In winter, betrothed to a temple ward
Heavy with the child of maybe Antipater
Fulfilling those prophesies of Edom and Israel
The heir of Adam, Abram, David and God

Were Joseph poor or humble
He would never have seen the stable
But cast out by the innkeeper
To deliver the child in a ditch by the roadside
Instead this proud head of household
Came to account for his tribe

Were Joseph poor or humble
He would never have heard of Heliopolis
Nor afforded to travel to Egypt
nor bring the Phoenix for rebirth
In this city of the radiant sun
To escape his uncle's rancour
And become the son of the sun ‹

Between the Lines ii
Mary

A virgin was not encumbered
In those peculiar days
With the baggage of chastity
Though the unseemly haste
From first blood to first blood
Left little time to freely lose
That precious maidenhead
If not already unfreely offered
To father or brother
Or for dower to this god or that
Well known in the multi-layered
Theology of temple mysteries
Irresistible to a meddling priest
Determined to enjoin Jesse to Edom
In one of many an ill starred attempt
To hothouse the prophesied Messiah
And bring about the end of the world ‹

Between the Lines iii
Mary

There is not one iota of evidence
For or against the notion
That Jesus son of Joseph
Pharisee, carpenter
Late of Nazareth
Was married
Yet I am tempted to ask
The price of sacrifice
Of a manifest god
Who freely eschewed
The essence of humanity
And left behind less
Than those millions
Slain in wars and by tyrants
To be enslaved and exploited

Those not so faint traces
Laced through a day
Determined and dedicated
To spring and motherhood
Place Mary the sister of Martha
Between Mother and Mortician
That in spite of the power of Jehova
The Goddess will have the last word. ◂

Between the Lines iv
Mary

The waning moon darkens
Each diminished night
Until only starlight rules
Deft hands wrap
A linen shroud around
The night cold body
And whispered prayers
Incant to ancient rhythms
Goddess blessed
To light the way away
From mortal life
Along a secret path
From whence so few return

She satisfied drifts
To blissful sleep
In the face of the rising sun ‹

Between the Lines v
Judas

This man is so reviled
For obedience to his lord
In setting the stage
An adulating cast of extra players
Palms and pot for breaking
On his master's cue
Ensuring that the upper room
With food and wine and bread
And the last ride was ready

Chief of staff
Master of ceremonies
Producer and director
Of this triumphant act
Who made quite sure
The High Priest and Sanhedrin
Followed the allotted script
From mark to mark

Yet it was his lord who strayed
Betraying them all
By his willing death
This chamberlain elect disgraced
By promises reneged
Turns to escape his vengeful clients
In the bliss of eternal sleep ‹

Between the Lines vi
Jesus

Death is the inevitable consequence of sin
and it is through sin that the Son of Man
Finds death

To a modern mind the assumption of sin
By a sinless man is more readily assumed
Than the transubstantiated host
That defeated Diana and Dionysus

Yet to an ancient theologian
There was no death without sin
Nor the resurrection miracle
Unless that life was forfeit for a cause

A life for life exchanged perhaps
A pact with nature to accept
The consequential death required
By God

The token sin required for death
The miracle of resurrection
And the inevitable translation
Required for this now sinless soul
Who could not die again ‹

Between the Lines vii
Paul

It was inevitable really
These pesky Christians
Righteous with goodness
And goodwill
Egalitarian even to women
Empowering the lowliest
Unafraid of death
Exulting in punishment
It had to stop!

It was a story worthy of the tabloids
Blindness
Miracles
Voices
Widows
Useful are widows
Symbols of virtue
Saul became Paul
And the ringer was in

Obey your man!
Cover your hair!
Do as you're told!
Blessed are no longer the meek
Or the hungry
Or the merciful
Or the poor
Because toilers who cannot toil
Or spinners who cannot spin
Are of no further use to the
God of Saul
To Bael
To mammon

Christians, reigned in
Made persecutors by
Their persecutors
A job well done
Unnoticed even after two millennia ‹

To My Rose

It may just be a window
Glazed to defeat the wind
Maybe the winter's snow
And sweet summer night's chill

Yet this window beaten
By the spring gales
Bright red paint sun scoured
Hides the heart of this stucco house

Suspended above the clay
Potted geraniums the village
Reflected in the afternoon sun
Hints at picturesque mystery

But the chastened stone frame
With fading wooden shutters
Of once brilliant poppy
Displays the bright comfortable soul within ‹

Birthday Star

A true star just shines
And from that selfless energy
Grows life in more myriad
Forms than we will ever know

The light of your star
Will truly inspire
Any who ever know you
To become stars themselves ‹

Colour

Red blue green orange
Lights bath your smiling face
Yellow blue red green
Bright eyes fixed gaze
Grey green orange blue
Dancing move to left and right
Blue teal green red
Reflect the buzzing refracted beat
Orange red yellow green
Happy and completely lost
Magenta black yellow red
Vibrating heart to jelly buzzed
Green yellow blue green
By burgeoning beat and also by me
Red blue yellow green again
I remember only your smiling face
Magenta red blue green orange yellow
And those eyes, those eyes fixed on me ‹

Colourful View

I see my world through Rose tinted spectacles
To some my view has a distinctly blue hue
While to others my planet is a dastardly red
But what my Rose really gave me at great personal cost
Were these cool yellow shades which sharpen my view
Disperse from my sight that glare which obscures
And brings into relief the things of great matter
Which most of us take as part of life's patter
Such as detail in cloud and the blades of the sward
Or do I see nature prepare to reward
Its tenants destructive of fittings provided
By sending the bailiffs of cold arctic ice
To scour out the closet to sand and repair
The surface exquisite of flora and fauna
And send us all packing in the fierce ozone free glare

Or am I just one of those antagonistic weirdoes
Who should be lined up against a wall and shot? ‹

I See You Here in Front of Me

I see you here in front of me
A face filled in with eyes and nose
Of flaws and light and shadow
Framed by falling tresses
Flowing over shoulders attached to arms
Of solid bone with hands and fingers too
Your breasts filled up to face that miasma
Of memory flowing over an
Expanding and contracting diaphragm
Giving life to an undulating stomach
Curving in turn through your red flamed pelvis
Touching that missing hip approaching down
Through thigh knee calf and foot
While counting one by one each tensile toe
I see you here in front of me
Not a jigsaw remembrance of moving parts
Chosen to suit that moment
Of lonely passion while cooking or cleaning
Or shopping or reading or making love
To your miasmic vision fading
In and out convenient and inconvenient
Response to craving touch or yearning clench
For now at least for now
I see you here in front of me ‹

Retratos
Self portrait

Here I am approaching middle age
that touch of youthful beauty
lost to looser lines and care worn eyes
To the discerning gaze
I am comfortable in my passion
wringing pleasure for any man or woman
prepared to challenge me
to set my libido free
My reflection oozes blood
a slash of exquisite pain
laying bare my wounded self
Take Me Hard
Hurt Me
Let Me Thrust and Scream
Let me take your hurt
and merge our ache
for in the morning I wear my
middle aged face again
hinting only to you
who has suffered too
just what I could do
The sharpness of my passion
lingering in the lines
loose upon my face ‹

Self portrait by Adriana Varejão
two paintings mounted on a corner
the second a perspective reflection of the first
with a cut from the forehead into the sky
wealing congealed blood

Plaint

I earn my living proudly on my back
Because that's the thing that I'm allowed to do
And no one can accuse me of a lack
Of gratitude, nor of failure to appreciate them too
And for that extra shilling I am even quite so willing
To fall upon my knees and play the bitch
Or to give them this mouth for filling
So I get extra billing
And if it's my arse they want: please make me rich
Because I have a child or three to keep and feed
And there's no one else at all to help me dress
Them not in rags to show the neighbours that I need
No charity from church or state
Nor from that girl from welfare I must impress

And when to journalist I tell my discontented tale
About the pimp; my shameful rape; and maybe compulsive
drugs
She, it's always she, her mouth agape and brow quite pale
Sucks up my story and cannot help but give me parting
hugs

Then when I read the story in the press
I am quite proud of my dexterous misdirection
For when I work to hide my mind's distress
My id's defended by skilful misperception

Because the awful truth of youth is very hard to tell
Of how I ran away one day from living hell
And like the whore next door and all the rest I know
Who found their father rather liked their cunt
Or uncle, brother, or even mother liked to hunt
Before the blood did flood my panties every month:
There's the men who hit and bit their wives
Then use their might to blight their children's lives.
It's from these daily treats to streets we safely go

How can you even think for one whole ghastly minute
That this is the life we truly dreamed about
And when we first left home so not so very long ago
To find a way to sleep quite safe at night
To feed ourselves and even go to school

Alas there is no way for this to happen
When politicians, to keep their precious vote,
Have deemed as sacred the nuclear familee
To send me back home, no thought at all of me,
I was too young to vote; nor will I pay the price
Demanded by the righteous just who from my lust to save
Insist I worship at my parent's feet
And beg forgiveness: they dare not ask
That very pregnant question they always should
Of who the father really is before forbidding to abort
Or why a child would ever want to leave
The safety of a loving home, free food
And the right to far too much tee vee

The answer is too painful to be heard
And will be deemed by all to be absurd
In any case I did not want to lose
To jail; and that child protection hell I'll not provoke
My loving siblings parents, and other folk,
Who are innocent of any sin because I choose
The safety of the streets where I repeat my rape.
For here, because I get to pick my johns, I really can
escape ⁊

Freda

I watched the faces
Looking at the faces of Freda
Predominately women
Some with her Hispanic brows
Seeing themselves look back
A stern aunt

I wondered, were I to paint
These many pretty faces
Which twitch or wrinkle
Would I select to tell their tale
This lip framing curl
Questing eye or fine lined frown
Shadows lighting life
Where none says none

Perhaps full unfledged faces
With perfect skin
Would lead my eye away
To curving breast of many sizes
Past the hips to well turned legs
Poised on points
Enclosed in awkward leather
Vivid skirts and scarves

What I will remember
Will be the faces
Faces of Freda and her friends
Faces watching Freda
And the eyes
Darting
Some fixed on paint and portrait
Others only on their lovers
Unaware of Diego's perfect portrait
Of his perfect self

Yet each and every one
In or out of love
Seeing and unseeing
Dressed or not
In stunning colour
Or defining black
Is watched
Forever
By Freda ‹

Moorchild

The moors were not their colourful selves today
Even though the sun shone bravely round the tall clouds
The hour was marked by hail and chilly squalls

Prancing lambs suggested mayhap it was spring
Curlews frantic called to guard their nests
Hid amongst the recent burnt dark heather

We walk across the springy re-grown heather base
Together toward a bleak standing stone
Amidst the noisy silence of sweeping isolation

There, together, alone, we left yet again
Another unformed child at the lonely foundation
Of this mossy ancient wayward marker
And in the bleak quiet, together, we loved. ‹

Realisation

We sat comfortably
Chastely
On the soft enfolding love seat
She barely larger than a child
Taut with anxiety
Proudly chattering of the things
She had done
Some of which tapped
Into her inner diffidence
Expressed with an
Unexpected maturity

He likes me to focus now
On our marriage
She enthused
To avoid distractions to
Our relationship
She explained

I contemplated the unasked questions
And unanswered untruths
She would tell
Sadness conveyed
Even as she earnestly smiled
Leaning forward in spite of
The chair's encompassing draw

I'm an old man I said
And one of the privileges of age
Is to speak my mind
I don't do it often
It's like a royal prerogative
Once exercised it's lost

I was silent

He is an arsehole I continued
But you knew he was an arsehole
Before you married him
For him you have set aside
That part of you that is interesting
Without that challenge from you
He will look elsewhere
For someone else to subjugate

Again I was silent

There was no change in her

Whatever you do...
Do not give him girl children

And still she did not react
And from somewhere deep inside
I realized
I was not telling her
Anything
She did not already know ‹

Gardening

Garden refuse, if not bagged
Immediately, tends to linger
Particularly if the bagger
Is not he or she who cut
So the only practical solution
Is to invite friends for dinner
Bagging then becomes one of those
Sunday Morning Zen things
After trooping down to SPAR
And the Sunday papers

My morning companions
A couple of busy blackbirds
Rooting about just a few feet away

I did nothing special
As I slashed away at the pile
Bending folding and cutting
Detritus into flimsy
Black bags

No submissive crouch talking
To an imaginary microphone
In a voice developed
For talking in dormitory
That crosses the room
Staying behind closed doors
As effective with prefects
As silverback gorillas

These two birds
Unconcerned and unafraid
Of the big hulking human
Waving ivy and creepers
Enthusiastically stuffing and clipping
And sweeping
To them I was just a big bird
Gathering big twigs for my nest ‹

The Egg

An egg alone sits amongst the heather
Nestling in a grassy bank, exposed
For all to see, except the wind,
Except the sun, except the mother,
Fated to be dinner for another
Sooner than its span dictates

It is in our nature to feel this loss
Mourn miscarriage or youthful misadventure

Projected to this nascent bird
Which, had it hatched and grown to fly,
Be taken by a hawk or gun
Grown to be taken by a larger brute
Or falling, failing on the wing, to feed
Five thousand, thousand myriad creatures
Which carry even we away in death

We are in truth no more than food
Except we leave a mark, except we teach,
Except we write, except we mother
Ideas and hope and love
Except we cannot see beyond our reason
Except we are no more ‹

Negative Capability

The Seraph indolent in the coruscating sun
Idly coiled and recoiled heating
Each flank in turn exposed to warmth's caress,
Relished in this fertile setting between two
Basking rivers, where amongst the reeds and osier
A single ancient pomegranate grows
Each fruit ripe and glowing red,
Casting a disturbing ever shifting shadow
Over the undulating coils loitering
Intently listening, watching, tasting, smelling.

Creatures skitter hither and thither
Sounding and resounding, feeding,
Grazing on the abundance of fruits and seeds
Unconcerned by the two two legged
Beings contained by the bounds of the rivers,
Tall amongst even the longest grasses,
Constrained by the abundant shoots
Turned by inconvenient coppices
Pausing now and then to reach into the thickets
For succulent sustenance, appearing
To glide from glade to glade.

The Seraph unravels and slips silently
Up amongst the ripe red alluring fruits
Winding round a rough knurled bough
Then a thought aloud, "Come, see this ripened fruit
Rich in sweet juice and cleansing bite"
Projects the Seraph, "Take and taste"
The woman stops, seeing the Seraph,
Starts, "Do not be afraid"
The Seraph beams extending its tail
To pluck and proffer the pregnant garnet.

The woman turns, reaching out warily to grasp
The rum fruit in her unsteady hand, in turn
Turns to the man.

The Grenade explodes: seeds and juice

Spurting all around bright red
Seeps through skin, their tongues
Taste the sweet sharp pulp;
Their minds burst with seminal awareness.

Knowing now their names, the harm of life giving sun
And the dangers all around, Eve weaves from leaves
And convenient reeds, shelter from the wet and cold
While Adam delves for the riches of the earth
And searches for the benevolent Deliverer:
The Seraph though was long gone
Sliding away to join the Seraphim
Rejoicing in heaven for their gift
Of knowledge and reason, the seeds
Of good and awareness of evil, the means to choose:
This treasure a gift to human kind
To further the purpose of creation.

Yet now this sacred gift the essential sin
All women blamed, punished, and enslaved,
Her blood malevolent, her wisdom garnished.
The endowment now is bound, contained, constrained,
Controlled, perverted means by which
This treasure is used to treasure earth
Implicit wealth worthied further than mere life
The power of poetry blunted by reason and prejudice
And away in heaven the Seraphim and Cherubim
Weep tears to swell the oceans
To drown the gift the Seraph on that clement day
So sweetly proffered
Such a long, long, time ago. ‹

*The Seraph, or Burning One, is a term used throughout the Old Testament to
refer to serpents, the name possibly derived from the effects of snake venom. The
snake is sacred throughout the ancient Middle East and often represents evil and
chaos; and equivocally, fertility, life and healing. The use of a fertility symbol in
the Garden of Eden is symbolic, especially as the interaction is with Eve: if Cain
were a 'Son of God' too, then he, God, brought Death in the murder of Abel and the
whole sequence can be linked to the cycle of life: the serpent swallowing its own
tail.

Keats' Walk

The meadow, pregnant with pools
Mislaid by winter floods
Gleams fresh green as sun fools
Us into summer cladding though chill blood

Briskly leads us along the sometime
Gravel path where the sometime lazy river
Flows fast past oak and lime
Willow beech birch and chestnut, a sliver

Of ripples betrays the awesome power
From water drawn beneath the palace, the castle
Garderobe, and here by the beck, a bower
Here a nesting swan, at times a rascal,

Settles above gleaming orbs of white
Cattle, boats in a sea of reeds,
Drift in their private eddies of light
Watching unseeing as waterfowl feeds

In the quieter corners where the millrace flows

From the now manicured fields clipped
For cricket, where once reserved for graze
Folk browsed; for herbs, or sipped
The air under the watchful gaze

Of the ancient tor of St. Catherine's Hill
In an eidetic eye one can truly see
A poet clamber beyond the mill
Absorbing colour along the lea

Engrossed with how he entire glows

Ambling briskly, or not, with friends, or not, until
To St. Cross he treads and then at tea is still. ‹

Liminal

John lived not quite in the City
Without the then missing Moorgate
Played with mates in the Moorfields
Under the watchful eyes from Bedlam
Never quite the citizen
Never quite the inmate
He built his own asylum

John worked not quite in the City
Without that gate that spans this river
His inmates now the Incurables
Who tutored by play in the theatre
In his hands are the bones of his patients
In his mind are the bones of his poesy
In that bridge are the bones of his Moorgate

John loved not quite in the City
First yearning for 'Bella by the seaside
Then cleaving to the familiar in Fanny
Joined by a wall and desire
Confined by a love he must abjure
Confined by disease and depression
He dreams now of Fanny and of martyrs

John died quite without his great City
His choice to eschew his Bright Stars
His excuse, his health and warm sun
Yet in truth he was settling his luxuries
Brooding on Fanny's bright beauty
Brooding on the hour of his death
His martyrdom the bones of asylum. ‹

Luxury

*"I have two luxuries to brood over in my walks, your
loveliness and the hour of my death."*
John Keats To Fanny Brawne, July 25th 1819.

The course of my daily comfort
Embraces the ample verdant growth
Thrusting lustrous from the loam
Wax green thirsting for the vital sun
Relieved by thriving coloured blooms
And flush budded engorged fruits.
Trees and vines wrestle
Together as needful of the one
As treacherous to the other
Contented in their embrace
As with their nesting flyers
A brooding hazard alert to peril
Awaiting their mate in ecstatic domesticity
Cleaving in rampant luxury
To establish the dislocation
Of the heart that cleaves for you.

In amongst the verdant stands
A naked bough stays forth
A lascivious limb stark
Thirsts neither for colour nor strains
To grasp the withering sun
Yet in the passing
Marks the place with permanence
A wisdom veiled
But within a place where insects breed
And creatures tryst in comfort
The coarse form an ugly beauty
Cleaving to be returned to loam
This separate branch
Of the heart that cleaves for you

We both know truly
That this love is a luxury
We can never rightly share
A dissolute dream
We cannot afford to found
This radiance which beams abundantly
Thrusts between us
A virile ditch
That makes us brood apart
And bars our breed
And will never let us serve
Together with those distractions
That make us unique
The consequence of my disorder
That cleaves your heart apart
From the heart that cleaves for you

Every wretched tread I take
Tells my heart
The tale of my impending end
The grasping gasp of thrusting growth
Thrills me with your loveliness
Each flower I pluck
A symbol of that which I cannot have
The wilting bloom a mark
Of that moment I will depart
A guilty relief from that lust
From what I am not let to choose
'Oh that I could have possession
Of them both at the same minute'
Together release me from my breath
To enjoy the dissolution
Of the heart that cleaves for you. ◄

Keats' House, Rome

In amongst the quiet stacks,
Locked against the casual loss
Of captured remembrance bound
In tooled leather, sewn
Into ordered cells,
Keys to be turned
For the panopticon
Not to become an oubliette,

Where the preserving gloom foretells
The approaching eve
Yet even with window and shutters
Closed against invading night
The sounds of the street
Rise reeking through the casements
Curl around the fastenings:
Lover's murmurings clip by
Children cry amazed
Amongst the street vendors' flamboyant wares
Opinion pretends for right,
Truth determined by volume
And pugilistic brash

Above it all *Summer Time*
Floats from a trumpet's bell
A mother's love singing
Knowledge to her children's hearts,
The cycle of seasons
The rhythm of rivers
Crop nurtured for reaping,
Absorbs the quiet library
Eddies through the cells
Of the turnkeys, riffling
For that elusive right
Lurking in the tomes of tombs
To be ordered into new
Bound and sinewed volumes

Cropped into controversy
Tied into fantastical wares
To occupy children
Confound lovers
And steal in turn through cracks
In the shutters and the edges of casements:
Our yield ‹

Red Dress

Posed
Poised
Perpendicular
Present, Purposeful
Protective eyes fearful
Plumed in red silk
Bristling
Brushing
Breathing
Blushing
Bowing, long, short, sharp
Sheathing
Fingers fretting, flaying
Padded
Placed
Plucked
Iridescent red
Flower
Flows
Tapping
Tap,   Tap
Taking
Triumphant
Silk surges red rivulets
Streams
Slaked
Sated
Sharp
Steady
Pizzicato
Plucking
Plucked
Presented
Poised
Posed
Placid
Pleased
Perfect ‹

Personal Landscape

The range of my personal landscape is changing
My territory, no longer familiar, subsumed
My call, no longer loud enough, to peal
Absorbed by trees with unfamiliar names
Coined from a fantastic lexicon of leviathans:
Here be Aviva, Aigon, Alveola, Santander;
Names bereft of the heft of trust;
Stripped of the comfort of familiarity;
And amongst whose branches it is no longer safe to climb.
For food, for succour, the simplest of things,
I have to leave my range, cross the territory of dragons
I am told is mine yet too far from home
For me to learn the turn of every knoll,
The form of every pathway,
And the risk of every shadow,
A land that is no longer mine
To love
While 'they'
Wonder why
I can no longer love
The landscape in which I live. ‹

Land With Opportunity

Whoever would believe
That JCBs or RB22s
Dumpers and mixers
Fences and portacabins
Could be things of beauty
But here etched in fine lines
White on black
Distanced compositions
Sparingly drawn
Displayed
Displacing walls
With stark beauty ⟨

*Based on a series of etchings
Land with Opportunity
by Catherine Sutcliffe-Fuller

What Will I Remember

What is it about today
That I would remember
Affectionately
Tomorrow?
How can this which is so bland
And functional
Compete?
My phone so ubiquitous palls against
A Philips Concert Hall Radio-Gramophone
On which I played Burl Ives
Or Listened with Mother,
Simulated bakelite curtains.
No flat pack furniture
Compares
With factory carved Croydon cabinets
While from my window
The French onion sellers,
Strings dangling from their
Bicyclette,
The rag and bone men
Perched on their horse drawn wagon,
"Rag and Bo...ne,
Rag and Bo...ne"!
The tinkers clad in pans
Pushing their prams with treasures.
In the quiet of the night
Amidst my Dinky cars
Triang trains
And Meccano monsters
Lit in the silver blue glow
Of an empty main road
An eerie silence punctuated
By the brisk click clack
Of occasional high heels
Unseen through the penny-farthing clad curtains.
So much more rememberable
Than the inebriate roamers

And procession of speeding taxis
Consoles of shoot-em-up games
And urgent texts from the kids next door.
Can this replace
Playing in fields with rusted iron artefacts
Hours of unsupervised fun
By ponds and riverbanks
Absorbing the changing seasons,
Their flora and fauna,
Needing only to be home in time for tea,
Iconic cars and 'planes
Replaced by clones
Identifiable only by the label on the back
Are our new heritage.

Is it this nostalgia
That makes me care for the land I live in
And is there enough
For my children to care for the land I left them? ‹

Exquisite

Exquisite!
Two notes
Beating together
One against the other
Passion
Complete and unfulfilled
Even with harmonic mitigation
Remains irresolute
A cut
Throbbing
With desire
For more
Or less
For something
Anything
Nothing
Exquisite ‹

Biography

Alan Gillott is poet, writer, composer, and singer who performs in the UK and USA and is well known throughout the North East. His most recent book is *Beyond the Window* (Fighting Cock Press); he has a following as a music and art critic and his poetry is known for its lyrical style based on internal structures. His observational poetry often highlights injustice and institutional irresponsibility.

He was born in Edinburgh to a Scottish mother and Yorkshire father from whence, at the tender age of six weeks, he was whisked off to live in Bury and from thence the Bowland Forest. He was educated mainly in Kent travelling between terms to Iraq and India. Though he started writing poetry as a teenager it wasn't until he was living in Dulwich, South London, that he met and was mentored by Alasdair Aston who instilled in him a love for form and the power of performance.

Alan's career took him throughout Europe, back to India and on to Singapore and Japan, with jobs based in various locations in the United States: in Pennsylvania, North Carolina, New York, New Jersey, Connecticut and Florida. In the USA he began featuring regularly at poetry venues and founded with his wife, Rose Drew, a popular open mic in Wilton Connecticut. Together they began publishing anthologies of their poets' best work under the imprint of Stairwell Books. Returning to England, Alan and Rose founded The Spoken Word open mic; they continue to publish anthologies and collections as a way of encouraging excellent but otherwise unpublished writing. Their success led to their taking on responsibility for the *Dream Catcher* literary journal.

His publication credits include poems in *The Nightcap Book*, Blue Dragon Press, *Community of Poets* Issue 20, the Connecticut Poetry Society's *Long River Run*, Turn of the River Press' *Wednesday at Curley's* and the University of Toledo's *Poems for Peace* Project. He has broadcast on cable TV, pirate radio, Radio Ryedale, University Radio York,

Chapel FM and Radio York. His book *Beyond the Window* is published by Fighting Cock Press.

He has participated in a number of collaborative projects including a Keats retrospective in Rome, participation in the TEDx programme, and developing a series of Poetry talk shows to be broadcast as podcasts. Alan also works with classical music composers as part of the *Sounds Lyrical Project* and his poems have been set by composers Edd Caine, David Power, David Lancaster, Peter Byrom-Smith, Tim Brooks and Steve Crowther and have been performed regularly in concert including part of York's long running Late Music Series.

Alan is also a musician who has been singing throughout his life, taking on the duties of Choirmaster at a number of churches, and where necessary writing the words and music for pieces to support the often depleted available resources. He has sung with London Welsh Choir, the London Symphony Orchestra Chorus, and at the Catholic basilicas in Brooklyn and Washington DC.

Recent publications available from Fighting Cock Press:

Fosdyke and Me And Other Poems, John Gilham
(with Stairwell Books)
Temporary Safety, Rose Drew
Dune Fox and Other Poems, Colin Speakman
Beyond the Window, Alan Gillott
Fishing for Spring, Mary Sheepshanks
Dancing blues to Skylarks, Mary Sheepshanks
Tales from a Prairie Journal, Rita Jerram
(with Stairwell Books)
50 : 50 – Celebrating Fifty Years of the Pennine Poets,
ed. Nicholas Bielby and Pauline Kirk (with Graft
Poetry)
People in a Landscape, Colin Speakman

For further information please contact

www.fightingcockpress.co.uk